The Economic and Political Essays of the Ante-bellum South

The Economic and Political Essays of the Ante-Bellum South

BY

ULRICH B. PHILLIPS

Reprinted from
THE SOUTH IN THE BUILDING OF THE NATION
(Volume VII)

THE SOUTHERN PUBLICATION SOCIETY
RICHMOND, VA.
1909

CHAPTER VIII

ECONOMIC AND POLITICAL ESSAYS IN THE ANTE-BELLUM SOUTH.

IN the ante-bellum period and for a generation afterward the Northern people and those of many European countries were profoundly concerned with liberalizing their social and economic institutions and with strengthening their national governments. But in the South the oppressive burden of the great race problem forced the body politic into social conservatism, and at the same time the necessity of insuring exemption from Northern control through Congressional majorities obliged the Southern leaders usually to antagonize nationalistic movements. The great world outside was radical in temper and nationalistic in policy; the South was conservative and stressed the rights of local units under the general government. The world measured the South by its current standards and found the South wanting. The world was not concerned with what the South had to say in its own behalf; it refused to read Southern publications and judged the South unheard. While alien and unfriendly views of the Old South abound to-day in huge editions, the conservative writings of Southerners to the manner born are mostly fugitive and forgotten. Yet on the whole, the Southern product of economic and political essays was very large, and in the mass these writings constitute a varied and often excellent body of literature, highly valuable as interpreting and recording the life and opinions of the successive generations.

As a rule these writings deal not with strictly economic or strictly political themes, but with complex public questions involving economics, politics and society simultaneously. They can be fitted into a plan of treatment only with difficulty and with some danger of slighting significant minor phases in some of the important essays discussed.

Theoretical and General Economics.

Economic theory is, of course, a development of quite recent growth. There was not much discussion of it in America in the ante-bellum period, and few Southerners, in particular, were closet philosophers enough to deal with its refinements. Some of the strongly edited newspapers, such as the *Federal Union* of Milledgeville, Ga., assigned columns regularly to "Political Economy," discussing theoretical questions in them at times, but filling them more generally with concrete items relating to industry and commerce at home and abroad. Among the college professors who wrote on economic themes, Thomas Cooper, long the dominant personality in South Carolina College, schooled a whole generation of budding statesmen in thorough-going *laissez-faire* economic doctrine; Thomas Dew, at William and Mary, and George Tucker, at the University of Virginia, appear to have taught political economy, without special bias, along with various other subjects in social and psychological fields, while J. D. B. DeBow, professor of political economy in the University of Louisiana at New Orleans, probably treated in his lectures more of concrete subjects of American industry and commerce than of unsubstantial theories. Each of these men might well have written general economic treatises, but Tucker and Cooper alone did so.

After a preliminary series of vigorous essays on

banking, public debts, population, etc., written in 1813 and collected into a volume in 1822, Tucker published a scholarly general treatise on money and banking in 1839, and a statistical analysis of the United States census returns in 1843. Cooper's only formal economic writing was his *Lectures on the Elements of Political Economy*, 1826, which embodied the current economic thought of the *laissez-faire* school. He, of course, advocated free trade and free banking. Incidentally, he estimated slave labor, under the existing conditions in the cotton belt, to be more expensive than free labor. Dew apparently published nothing noteworthy except his famous essay on slavery, 1833, while DeBow contented himself with editing his *Review* and a cyclopedic description of Southern and Western resources in 1853-54, superintending the eighth United States census, writing a compendium of that census, 1854, and issuing occasional articles on the plantation system and the project of reopening the foreign slave trade. Aside from the writings of these few professional economic philosophers, the South produced practically nothing in economic theory or in formal statistics. Robert Mills' *Statistics of South Carolina*, 1826, and George White's *Statistics of Georgia*, 1849, were mere historical and descriptive miscellanies.

Agriculture.

Few Southerners were pen-and-ink men by native disposition. Most of them wrote for publication only under the pressure of public emergency. In easy times the reading class of Southerners would read the ancient and modern European classics, and the local newspapers would be concerned mainly with world politics. But in times of industrial crises thinking men would inquire for economic and social treatises throwing light upon American problems;

the newspapers would teem with essays on the causes, character and remedies of the existing depression, and the job-presses would issue occasional books and numerous pamphlets by local authors upon the issues of the day.

In Southern agriculture each occurrence of a crisis brought forth substantial writings, whether soil surveys, descriptions of methods, or didactic essays. Near the end of the Eighteenth century, for example, occurred a severe depression in Carolina coast industry, and in 1802 appeared Drayton's *View of South Carolina,* describing methods and improvements in indigo, rice and cotton, and in 1808 Ramsay's *History of South Carolina* was published, with a large appendix full of agricultural data from and for the sea-island district. During the War of 1812 tobacco was heavily depressed, and John Taylor, of Caroline, began to write his *Arator* essays for newspaper and pamphlet publication. In the late twenties the Eastern cotton belt felt the pinch of Western competition, and in 1828 was established at Charleston the *Southern Agriculturist,* a strongly edited monthly which was well supported by subscribers and contributors for several years until the return of easy times. From 1839 to 1844 was the most severe economic depression in the history of the ante-bellum South. Cotton was principally affected, but all other interests suffered in sympathy. The result was an abundant activity in economic writing, agriculture included. Edmund Ruffin, who had long been conspicuous as a soil and crop expert in Virginia, was employed by the commonwealth of South Carolina to make an agricultural survey of the state, made his first descriptive report in 1843, and published occasional essays and addresses during the next decade upon soils and fertilizers. R. F. W. Allston, a sea-island planter, published in 1843 a memoir on rice planting (as well as a general descriptive essay in 1854 on Southern seacoast crops), and in 1844 Whitemarsh B. Seabrook, president of the South Carolina Agricultural Society, afterward governor of the state, published a memoir upon the development of sea-island cotton culture.

All of these publications were soon eclipsed in importance by the establishment of the famous and invaluable *DeBow's Review* at New Orleans in 1846, which for many years afterward not only abounded in contributed articles and news items upon agricultural and other economic subjects, but also reprinted most of the noteworthy fugitive addresses and essays which appeared in the field of Southern economics during the period of the *Review's* publication. The *Cotton Planters' Manual*, compiled by J. A. Turner, of Georgia (1857), deserves mention as a collection of useful essays reprinted from various sources on cotton culture, plant diseases, manures and commerce. On the sugar industry, nothing was written in the United States of value comparable to several essays in the West Indies: Clement Caines, *Letters on the Cultivation of the Otaheite Cane* (London, 1801), the anonymous *Practical Rules for the Management and Medical Treatment of Negro Slaves in the Sugar Colonies* (London, 1803), and M. G. Lewis' *Journal of a West India Proprietor* (London, 1834).

Mining, Manufactures, Transportation and Commerce.

Upon the subject of mining, all Southern colonial and ante-bellum literature is negligible after the time of William Byrd's excellent description of the Virginia iron mines about 1732. West Virginia salt, Tennessee copper and Georgia gold were neglected by all but newspaper writers, while Carolina phosphates, Alabama iron, Louisiana sulphur and Texas oil did not begin to be mined until after the antebellum period.

On manufactures, William Gregg published a series of articles in the *Charleston Courier* and collected them in a pamphlet, 1845. He described the prior attempts at textile manufacturing in South Carolina, attributing their ill-success to the smallness of the scale of operation and the failure of each mill to specialize in a single sort of cloth; and he urged more extensive embarkation upon manufacturing and the avoidance of past errors. Aside from factory officials in their company reports and occasional descriptive, apologetical and hortatory writers in *DeBow's Review,* Gregg, with his slender writing, seems to have been alone in the field.

In the field of transportation there were innumerable essays and reports upon local problems, projects and progress in the improvement of transit facilities. Among them the treatise of Robert Mills on a project of public works in South Carolina, 1822, is notable for its elaboration and pretentiousness and for the complete impracticability of his plans. Robert Y. Hayne's essays and reports on the Charleston and Cincinnati railroad project, 1837-39, were similarly chimerical, as were also some of the Alabama writings on plank roads about 1850. To offset the recklessness of such writings as these, an anonymous writer published a notable series of ultra-conservative essays in the *Charleston Mercury* and collected them in a pamphlet, *The Railroad Mania, By Anti-Debt,* Charleston, 1848. In the main the Southern essays in the field of transportation were distinctly sane and well reasoned. Some of the official railroad reports are distinctly valuable as noting general economic developments in their territory year by year. Among such are the reports of the Central of Georgia officers, which were collected and reprinted by the company in occasional volumes.

The genius of the Southern people ran very slightly to commerce, and their literature shows little attention to any but a few of its spectacular features. The principal themes attracting the newspaper and periodical writers (and there were practically no others dealing with commerce) were the importance of cotton in the world's commerce, the possibility of cornering the cotton supply or otherwise manipulating its price in the interest of the producers, the project of establishing direct trade in steamship lines between Southern ports and Europe, and thereby attempting to reduce the Northern profits on Southern commerce, and the possibility of reopening the African slave trade. The cotton trade discussions were most conspicuous about 1836 to 1839, the study of foreign commercial relations was mainly in the fifties, and the debate over the slave trade was waged, between a few advocates and numerous opponents, between 1855 and 1861.

Labor.

White wage-earning labor was probably not so extremely scarce in the ante-bellum South as most historians would have us believe, but trades-unions were few, and the labor problems apart from negroes and slavery were not conspicuous enough to occasion the writing of many formal essays. Joseph Henry Lumpkin, later chief justice of Georgia, published, in 1852, an essay, *The Industrial Regeneration of the South,* which gives his interpretation of existing conditions, incidentally, in his somewhat utopian argument in favor of manufactures. He says, in part:

"It is objected that these manufacturing establishments will become the hotbeds of crime * * * But I am by no means ready to concede that our poor, degraded, half-fed, half-clothed and ignorant population, without Sabbath schools, or any other kind of instruction, mental or moral, or without any just appreciation of character,—will be injured by giving them employment, which will bring them under the oversight of employers who will inspire them with self-respect by taking an interest in their welfare."

The pros and cons of employing free labor for plantation work were discussed in newspaper articles, but probably the best journalistic item in this connection is that of the traveler-scientist, Charles Lyell, written in 1846 and published in his *Second Visit to the United States* (Vol. II., p. 127):

"The sugar and cotton crop is easily lost if it is not taken in at once when it is ripe * * * Very lately a planter, five miles below New Orleans, having resolved to dispense with slave labor, hired one hundred Irish and German emigrants at very high wages. In the middle of the harvest they all struck for double pay. No others were to be had, and it was impossible to purchase slaves in a few days. In that time he lost produce to the value of ten thousand dollars."

Negroes.

The Southerners of the plantation districts were as familiar with the typical plantation negroes as they were with typical cows and horses. Thomas Jefferson, in his *Notes on Virginia* (Query 14), characterized negroes as improvident, sensuous, inconstant, well endowed in memory, poor in reasoning power and dull in imagination. Few, aside from Jefferson, thought it necessary to describe the obvious. In the West Indies, where for many decades the volume of slave imports was enormous and where the fresh Africans were representative of all the diverse tribes from Senegal and Abyssinia to Good Hope and Madagascar, the planters were prompted to compare the tribal traits and thus to publish discussions of negro characteristics in general. But in the continental South, in the antebellum period, the tribal stocks, Berber, Coromantee, Ebo, Congo, Kaffir, Hottentot, etc., had become blended into the relatively constant type of the American plantation negro. As a familiar item in the white man's environment, the negro was not to be described or interpreted, but was rather to be accepted and adjusted. Dr. J. C. Nott, of Mobile, at the middle of the Nineteenth century, like Mr. F. L. Hoffman at the end of it, was led to study and publish upon negro traits by reason of his interest in life insurance. Dr. S. A. Cartwright, of New Orleans, in the same period as Nott, was led into a general study of the negro by his interest in negro diseases. Practically all the other writers approached the subject of the negro as a corollary to the question of the perpetuity of slavery. Dr. J. H. Van Evrie, of Washington, later of New York, voiced the dominant opinion when he wrote (1853) that the ills of the South were mainly attributable not to slavery, but to the negro. In 1861 Van Evrie further elaborated his unflattering opinion of the negro in his book, *Negroes and Slavery,* which he reprinted in 1867 with the title, *White Supremacy and Negro Subordination.* Van Evrie, as usual with controversialists, falls into the error of proving too much.

In the case of anti-slavery writers, whether Northern or Southern, it required the abolition of slavery to reveal the negro as a concrete phenomenon. H. R. Helper was the most extreme example of this. His *Impending Crisis* (1857) denounced the institution of slavery with the greatest vigor as the cause of all the Southern ills, but his *Nojoque* (1867) was devoted to a still more absurdly extreme denunciation of the negro as a worthless encumbrance and a curse. It is curious that extremely little was published upon the mulatto element, except a few essays upon the orthodox but indefensible theme that by reason of their shortness of life, their infertility and their moral degeneracy, the mixed breed formed a negligible though vicious fraction of the population.

Slavery.

The economic and social aspects of slavery furnished a bulk of essays only equalled in the South by that upon the political bearings of the same institution of domestic servitude. In the colonial period the discussion was abundant, sane, and matter-of-fact, so far as may be judged from indirect evidence, but little of it went into print. In the period of the Revolution the discussion was so hysterical in tone that it resulted at the South more in reaction than in liberalism.

The great ante-bellum debate on the subject brought forth an extreme variety of essays, both as to scope and tone, but the general inclination of the writers, with the notable exception of Helper, was to confront conditions, not theories. Before 1833 the discussion in the South tended to be a humdrum rehashing of time-honored views, relieved by an occasional reflection of the ideas of the European economists. James Raymond wrote an essay on the *Comparative Cost of Free and Slave Labor in Agriculture* in 1827, which was awarded a prize by the Frederick County, Maryland, Agricultural Society. His argument follows the line of Adam Hodgson's reply to J. B. Say's discarded early views: the farmer needs an elastic supply of labor, and hireling labor is suited for this while slave labor is not; slaves are lazy, slipshod, wasteful, as contrasted with the carefulness, efficiency and frugality of freemen. Raymond, of course, like the typical abolitionist, divorced the slavery issue from the negro issue by ignoring the question of what would become of the great mass of Southern negroes when freed. Raymond also ignored the fact that in the principal Southern industries, under the plantation system, regularity was more to be desired than elasticity in the labor supply, and that slavery secured the desired constancy in the number of laborers available. The publication of Professor Dew's famous essay in 1833, prompted by the debate upon projects for abolition in the Virginia legislature in 1831-32, demonstrated that the slavery question was essentially a phase of the great negro question. After censuring the recklessness of the Virginia debate, and showing that slavery had been a highly serviceable institution in furthering human progress in many countries and in many centuries, Dew analyzes the American situation and the proposals for its betterment. He condemns the several plans, varying in detail, for the emancipation and deportation of the negroes on the grounds of the excessive cost of the process, the threatened paralysis of plantation industry, and the inability of the negroes to maintain their own welfare if deported to Africa. He condemns still more strongly all plans for abolition which do not include provision for deportation, pointing out the social and industrial dangers of freeing an irresponsible population, and pointing to the record of the Northern free negroes and to the chaotic state of affairs in Hayti as warnings. After Dew's essay no writer could secure countenance in the South for any anti-slavery plans unless he could show some means of readjusting the negro population in a way not endangering the security of the whites or threatening the general welfare.

In close harmony with Dew's argument, essays were written in the thirties and forties by Chancellor William Harper and Gov. J. H. Hammond, both of South Carolina, which were reprinted in 1852 along with Dew's essay and a slender one by W. G. Simms, in a volume entitled the *Pro-Slavery Argument*. Harper, following Dew's theme in general, lays main stress upon the civilizing and tranquilizing effects of slavery. Hammond's essay, written in the form of a reply to Thomas Clarkson's attacks upon slavery, is an exceptionally strong apology for the institution. He concedes that slave labor is expensive, by reason of the slave's first cost and the expense of feeding, clothing and sheltering him and his family in infancy, sickness and old age, in bad seasons as well as good; and he prophesies that any great increase in the density of population will cause the abandonment of slavery by making free labor available and cheaper. Meanwhile, in view of the sparseness of the Southern population and the unfitness of the negroes for the stress of competition, he deprecates any radical readjustments and resents extraneous interference.

Numerous other Southern essayists clamored for public attention, of whom only the more significant can here be noted. John Fletcher, of Louisiana, in 1851 issued a bulky primer to prove the goodness of slavery, in easy lessons and with main reference to Holy Writ. George S. Sawyer, also of Louisiana, gave an elaborate eulogy of slavery upon historical and ethical grounds in his *Southern Institutes* (1859). Henry Hughes, in pamphlets of 1858-59, tried to bolster up slavery by the euphemistic device of changing its name to warranteeism, and thereby indicating that its purpose was to maintain industrial order rather than to exploit the laboring class; but Hughes could not get an audience even in the South for his ineffective plea. Daniel Christy, of Cincinnati, entitling his book *Cotton is King* (1855), magnified the economic efficiency and vital importance of slavery as a divinely established institution. Though Christy may not have been a Southerner, his book was adopted by the Southern ultramontanists as their own. Professor A. T. Bledsoe, of the University of Virginia, in his book *An Essay on Liberty and Slavery* (1856), endeavored to refute seventeen specific fallacies of the abolitionists, and to vindicate slavery and all its works, including the fugitive slave law. In 1860 E. N. Elliott, "President of Planters' College, Mississippi," bought the authors' rights to Christy's and Bledsoe's books, secured new scriptural arguments for slavery from Dr. Stringfellow, of Virginia, and Dr. Hoge, of New Jersey, and an ethnological essay from Dr. Cartwright, of New Orleans, added to these Hammond's and Harper's already standard essays, and the text of the Dred-Scott decision by the United States Supreme Court, printed the whole in one bulky subscription volume, *Cotton is King and Pro-Slavery Arguments* (1860), and sold it in great numbers to the planters and townsmen on the eve of the war. The book, on the whole, compares very unfavorably with the more modest but substantial *Pro-Slavery Argument* of 1852.

More notable as a contribution to thought are the two books by George Fitzhugh, of Virginia, with the curious titles: *Sociology for the South, or the Failure of Free Society* (1854), and *Cannibals All, or Slaves Without Masters* (1857). Declaring himself an outright socialist, Fitzhugh denounces the whole modern system of wage-labor, and contends that laborers on hire are subject to more severe exploitation than laborers in bondage. He advocates benevolent despotism on general principles, and particularly where applied to a class so little capable of self-protection as the negroes in America. He holds up the Southern plantation system for the admiration of all socialists, communists, or other paternalists. Fitzhugh, however, injures the effect of his books by his own loquacity. He adds chapters at random championing the South against the North in every possible connection, and thereby lets it seem, whether justly or not, that he is a socialist only for the sake of the argument.

As an assault upon the general position held by the whole group of writers above treated, Hinton R. Helper, of North Carolina, issued his startling book, *The Impending Crisis of the South* (1857). He points out the relative economic stagnation in the South, asserts that slavery is its sole cause, and denounces the slave-holding class as a cruel and wicked oligarchy conspiring for the oppression of the negroes and non-slave-holding whites alike. Helper is a past master in the art of leaping at conclusions and concealing the feat by outbursts of perfervid rhetoric. Helper was the spokesman of a group of radical Southern non-slaveholders, but he secured relatively little Southern endorsement on the whole because he failed to meet adequately the vital problem of what to do with the negro population in the event of the abolition of slavery. But the North bought fifty thousand copies in three years, and at the North, where Helper's *Nojoque* has always been unknown, his *Impending Crisis* is still considered by thousands to be the soundest of interpretations.

Daniel R. Goodloe, of North Carolina, was a much more substantial though less glittering opponent of slavery. In his pamphlet of 1846, *Inquiry Into the Causes Which Have Retarded the Accumulation of Wealth and Increase of Population in the Southern States,* he presented most of the data which Helper used ten years later, along with some interpretations which were too deep for Helper to grasp. To the time-honored criticism that slavery hampered industrial progress by stigmatizing labor, Goodloe added a thought which he had worked out that a still more important phase of the burdensome character of slavery lay in its devoting a huge volume of capital to the purchase and control of laborers. He showed that by buying laborers instead of hiring them the South had long been sinking money and depriving itself of resources which might have been used to great advantage in the development of large-scale manufacturing and commerce.

The final ante-bellum word upon the burdensomeness of slavery and its actual and prospective decadence was written by George M. Weston, who seems to have come from Maine and lived mostly in Washington, and at Washington to have gotten into sympathetic touch with the clearest thinkers on slavery, and also to have read well a wide variety of pertinent literature. In his book, *The Progress of Slavery in the United States* (1857), he shows the relatively stagnant condition of the slave-holding communities, discussing the reasons therefor, he points out the encroaching of the free-labor system within the border of the slave-holding section, prophesying a still further restriction by economic process of the area and importance of slave-holding industry, he demonstrates that the then current agitation for the congressional increase of slave-holding territory was purely political in character and offered no economic advantage to the captains of industry in the active plantation districts, and he foretells that the decadence and disappearance of slavery will inure to the benefit instead of the injury of the South. To the careful student of Southern history it may well appear that Weston's little-known book was more representative of the views of well-informed and thoughtful Southerners than were the manifestoes of the politicians. In those years of excited controversy just preceding the war, public opinion in the South, of course, opposed any revision of opinions in the face of the enemy. Public expressions of doubts as to the perfect efficiency and goodness of the slavery system were discouraged at the time. But there is little doubt that many substantial Southerners held many of the views which Hammond, Goodloe and Weston expressed. Among the evidences of this may be cited the essays of representative keen Southern students of the following generation, who it is most reasonable to suppose expressed much of what had existed, even though the ideas may have been latent, in the minds of thoughtful men in the ante-bellum years. Among the essays in point may be mentioned: W. L. Trenholm, *The Southern States, Their Social and Industrial History, Conditions and Needs,* published in the Transactions of the American Social Science Association for September, 1877, and J. C. Reed, *The Old and New South* (1876), reprinted in the Appendix to the same author's *The Brother's War* (1905).

Social Surveys.

As a general treatise upon social types, D. R. Hundley's *Social Relations in Our Southern States* (1860) stands alone among the productions of Southern writers. Born in the South, the author says his education "was chiefly acquired at Southern institutions of learning, in the states of Alabama, Tennessee, Kentucky and Virginia," and was completed by a course in law at Harvard. His collegiate migrations would indicate a waywardness of disposition somewhat characteristic of well-to-do Southern youth in the period, and his waywardness crops out at many places where flippant digressions and gibes at the North mar the character of his book. Nevertheless, Hundley was widely traveled, closely observant, keen in analysis and facile in characterization, and his book is valuable accordingly. His chapters on the Southern gentleman, the Southern middle class, the Southern yeoman, the poor-white and the cotton snob, as he calls the *nouveau riche* of the South, are particularly useful contributions. He gives good fragmentary data, also, upon student dissipation, upon slave traders and upon negro conditions generally, including a notice of the social distinctions which prevailed among the slaves.

William Gilmore Simms, in his *Southward Ho* (1854), gives informal sketches of society in Virginia and the Carolinas, from the point of view of one who was at the same time a middle-class South Carolinian and a citizen of the world. Joseph Baldwin's *Flush Times of Alabama* (1853), a semi-humorous work, is the chief writing upon society in the Southwest.

Political Essays; Theoretical.

Southern writings upon the abstract theory of government were as scarce as we have seen those to have been in theoretical economics. Practically all state papers are negligible as essays in political theory, including Jefferson's Declaration of Independence and Mason's Virginia Bill of Rights, for each of these was merely a brilliantly phrased set of ideas borrowed from current European philosophy, and applied concretely to interpret and justify the American problems and policy of the moment. The writings of Francis Lieber, notable as they are, ought hardly to be claimed as of Southern production, for although Lieber was a professor in South Carolina College for many years and wrote all of his principal books there, he never ceased to be an alien in the Southern country. With his mind always dominated by German idealistic devotion to liberty and revolution, he could feel nothing but repugnance at the conditions in the midst of which he sojourned and at the philosophy of the people who, against his preference, were his neighbors. Lieber's books would indicate that he never confronted any of the distinctive Southern problems of concrete racial adjustments. There remain for mention here only St. George Tucker and John C. Calhoun, each of whom had the United States constitution conspicuously in mind when writing upon government in general, and each of whom was a full-fledged product and a spokesman of the Southern community. Tucker's essay, published as an appendix to his edition of Blackstone's *Commentaries* (1803), championed the Eighteenth century doctrine of inherent rights and the social compact, and applied it elaborately in interpreting the Federal system of the United States. By correlating the position of the states in the Federal compact with the position of individuals in the theoretical social compact, he, of course, provided a basis for reasoning out the supremacy of the states and the subordinate character of the central government. He proceeded to state expressly as an inevitable deduction from his general scheme of political philosophy, that the several states had an indefeasible right of seceding from any Federation or Union which they had entered or might enter.

Calhoun organized his formal writing in political philosophy into two treatises written shortly before his death. Of these, the *Disquisition on Government* (1851), as Professor W. A. Dunning has well said, "is in some respects the most original and the most profound political essay in American literature. It is by no means a complete philosophy of the state, nor is its relation to the concrete issues of the day much disguised; but it penetrates to the very roots of all political and social activity, and presents, if it does not satisfactorily solve, the ultimate intellectual problems in this phase of human existence.'' In bald outline the thread of the essay is as follows: Society is necessary to man, and government is necessary to society; but governments tend to infringe upon the just liberties and rights of individuals, and popular governments are no less prone toward this oppression than are monarchies, for the reason that popular majorities are prone to consider their own interests as the only ones which the government ought to promote, and prone accordingly to ignore and override the interests and rights of minorities. The suffrage franchise alone will not safeguard the individual against oppression. Just as governments are instituted to secure the weak against the strong, constitutions are established in large part to restrain the governments when controlled by strong interests from overriding minority rights. To limit the government properly in this regard without unduly weakening it is a most delicate and difficult problem, and one which the framers of the American Federal constitution did not fully solve. This is the profound problem as seen by Calhoun. His prescription of a remedy is less strong than his diagnosis of the trouble. He proposes a system of concurrent majorities by which each great interest in the country should be put into control of one branch of the legislative power of the government, and thereby be given a veto power upon measures proposed by each other great interest. Calhoun's plan is not fully adequate for the solution of the problem, but neither is any other plan ever yet devised by any philosopher or any nation.

Constitutional Construction.

Whenever in Federal politics of the ante-bellum period a majority in Congress overrode the opposition, or was about to override it, upon an important issue, it was a fairly constant practice for the spokesman of the minority to appeal to the constitution and declare the programme of the majority to be an exercise by the Government of unwarranted powers. The majority, of course, could often ride rough-shod and had little need of resorting to pamphlets and treatises to defend its constitutional position. Quires were written in championship of broad construction, but reams for strict construction; and it happened that most of strict construction writers were men of the South. Madison's articles in the *Federalist* may be dismissed as being devoted to explanation and eulogy rather than to the construction of the constitution. Madison soon reacted from his nationalistic position and wrote the Virginia Resolutions (1798), which, with Jefferson's Kentucky Resolutions, adopted in minority remonstrance against the Alien and Sedition acts of Congress, served for many years as the official embodiment of constitutional construction for the state-rights school. Shortly afterward, in 1803, John Marshall began his series of vigorous nationalistic decisions which averaged more than one per year for the next thirty years, accompanying the decisions of his court in most of these cases with fulminations from his own pen to preach the doctrines of broad construction. Henry Clay, who, aside from Webster, was the principal other spokesman in the United States for broad construction, contributed no arguments of note upon constitutional topics, but confined himself largely to arguments on the grounds of expediency, making special use of the *argumentum ad hominem*. The several steps taken by Marshall and Clay gave the chief occasions for the publication of strict construction arguments by the opposing school. The principal essayists who were spurred immediately by Marshall were the Virginians, Spencer Roane and John Taylor, of Caroline. Roane, who as chief justice of Virginia had the chagrin of seeing some of his own state-rights decisions reversed by Marshall's court on appeal, resorted to the public press in remonstrance. His principal series of articles was printed in the *Richmond Inquirer* in May-August, 1821, and collected in a pamphlet entitled *The Letters of Algernon Sidney.* Taylor issued a succession of polemical books: *Inquiry Into the Principles and Policy of the Government of the United States* (1813), expressing his disrelish of the consolidation tendencies of the time; *Construction Construed* (1820), denouncing the McCulloch *vs.* Maryland decision and asserting the sovereignty of the states; *Tyranny Unmasked* (1822), denying the power of the Federal Supreme Court to assign limits to the spheres of state and Federal authority, and advocating a state veto for emergency use in curbing Federal encroachment, and *New Views of the Constitution* (1823), which reiterated his former contention and stressed the value of the states as champions of sectional interests against injury by hostile congressional majorities.

Clay's campaign for his "American System" drew fire mainly from the South Carolinians. In 1827 Robert J. Turnbull, under the pseudonym of Brutus, published a series of thirty-three articles in the *Charleston Mercury,* and promptly issued them in a pamphlet entitled *The Crisis: Or Essays on the Usurpation of the Federal Government,* which he dedicated "to the people of the 'Plantation States' as a testimony of respect, for their rights of sovereignty." Turnbull vehemently urged the people of the South to face the facts, to realize that the North was beginning to use its control of Congress for Southern oppression by protective tariffs and otherwise; and he proposed as a remedy that South Carolina should promptly interpose her own sovereignty and safeguard Southern interests by vetoing such congressional acts as she should decide to be based upon Federal usurpations and intended for Northern advantage at the cost of Southern oppression. McDuffie and Hayne promptly assumed the leadership of the state-sovereignty-and-Southern-rights cause in Congress and many other prominent South Carolinians fell in line, including the editors R. B. Rhett and J. H. Hammond, and including most conspicuously John C. Calhoun, who drafted nearly all the state papers of South Carolina during the nullification episode, and who, in addition, issued powerful memorials upon the issues of the day over his own signature. These writings are too prominently a part of American history to require any detailed discussion here.

The final issue prompting state sovereignty expressions was that of negro slavery. The principal work in this group was Calhoun's *Discourse on the Constitution and Government of the United States* (1851), which supplements his *Disquisition on Government*, already outlined. This *Discourse* follows the theme of his more general *Disquisition*, applying its contentions more specifically to the American Federal problem; it champions concurrent majorities again, champions the historical doctrine of state sovereignty and defends, in somewhat subdued phrase, his former pet plan of nullification. The *Discourse* and the *Disquisition* were Calhoun's political testament; the great obituary of the state sovereignty and secession movement was Alexander

H. Stephens' *Constitutional View of the War between the States,* which, as a post-bellum work, falls beyond our present scope.

Party Politics.

It was the custom of but a few leaders to address their constituents for party purposes through essays instead of from the hustings. One of these was Robert Goodloe Harper, who, upon his retirement from Congress in 1801, addressed to his South Carolina constituents a eulogistic but sane and vigorous memoir upon the constructive work of his party: *A Letter Containing a Short View of the Political Principles of the Federalists, and of the Situation in Which They Found and Left the Government.* Another was Edward Livingston, who, when asking for reëlection to Congress in 1825, issued an *Address to the Electors of the Second District of Louisiana,* which is notable for his attempt to reconcile the desire of the sugar planters for protection to their own industry with the disrelish of the cotton planters for the policy of protection in general, by the device of calling the duty on sugar a revenue item and not a protective item in the tariff schedules. Various other candidates, of course, issued electioneering pamphlets, practically all of which are negligible as essays. On a plan combining an historical sketch with political propaganda were several writings such as Thomas Cooper's *Consolidation: An Account of Parties in the United States, from the Convention of 1787 to the Present Period* (1824), written, of course, with a state-rights purpose; Henry A. Wise's *Seven Decades of the Union,* eulogizing John Tyler and the policy of the state-rights Whigs, and such biographies as J. F. H. Claiborne's *Life and Correspondence of John A. Quitman* (1860), which contains secession propaganda on the author's own account along with the biography of Quitman.

Sectionalism.

Instead of making a catalogue of the many essays which deal with petty sectionalism within the several states and with grand sectionalism between the North and the South, we will conclude our view of economic and political writings by presenting the theme of William H. Trescott's *The Position and Course of the South* (1850), as an embodiment of the soundest realization of the sectional conditions and prospects of the Southern section in the closing decade of the ante-bellum period. The author, a leading, experienced, conservative citizen of South Carolina, states in his preface, dated Oct. 12, 1850, that his purpose is to unify the widely separated parts of the South. He says his views are not new, but they are characteristically Southern: "We are beginning to think for ourselves, the first step toward acting for ourselves." The essay begins with an analysis of industrial contrasts. He says that in the slavery system the relation of capital and labor is moral—labor is a duty, in the wage-earning system the relation is legal—the execution of contract. The contract system, he says, promotes constant jealousy and friction between capital and labor, while the slavery system secures peace by subordinating labor to capital. The political majority of the North represents labor; that of the South, capital; the contrast is violent. Free labor hates slave labor, and will overturn the system if it can. The two sections with many contrasting and conflicting characteristics are combined under the United States constitution, but they are essentially irreconcilable. Even in foreign relations the North is jealous of foreign powers for commercial and industrial reasons, while Southern industry is not competitive with, but complementary to European industry and commerce, and the South, if a nation by itself, would be upon most cordial terms with foreign powers. "The United States government under the control of Northern majorities must reflect Northern sentiment, sustain Northern interests, impersonate Northern power. Even if it be conceded that the South has no present grievance to complain of, it is the part of wisdom to consider the strength and relations of the sections, and face the question, what is the position of the South? In case our rights should be attacked, where is our constitutional protection? The answer is obvious. If the expression of outraged feeling throughout our Southern land be anything but the wild ravings of wicked faction, it is time for the South to act firmly, promptly and forever. But one course is open to her honor, and that is secession and the formation of an independent confederacy. There are many men grown old in the Union who would feel an honest and pardonable regret at the thought of its dissolution. They have prided themselves on the success of the great American experiment of political self-government, and feel that the dissolution of the Union would proclaim a mortifying failure. Not so. The vital principle of political liberty is representative government, and when Federal arrangements are discarded, that lives in original vigor. Who does not consider the greatest triumph of the British constitution the facility and vigor with which, under slight modifications, it developed into the great republican government under which we have accomplished our national progress. And so it will be with the United States constitution. The experiment of our fathers will receive its highest illustration, and a continent of great republics, equal, independent and allied, will demonstrate to the world the capabilities of republican constitutional government. We believe that Southern interests demand an independent government. We believe that the time has now come when this can be established temperately, wisely, strongly. But in effecting this separation we would not disown our indebtedness, our gratitude to the past. The Union has spread Christianity, fertilized a wilderness, enriched the world's commerce wonderfully, spread Anglo-Saxon civilization. "It has given to the world sublime names, which the world will not willingly let die—heroic actions which will light the eyes of a far-coming enthusiasm. It has achieved its destiny. Let us achieve ours."

BIBLIOGRAPHY.—Acton, Lord: *The Civil War in America* (1866, reprinted as Chap. IV. of his *Historical Essays and Studies*, London, 1907); Allston, R. F. W.: *Memoir of the Introduction and Planting of Rice in South Carolina* (Charleston, 1843), and *Sea-Coast Crops of the South* (1854, reprinted in *DeBow's Review*, XVI., 589-615); Baldwin, Jos. G.: *The Flush Times of Alabama and Mississippi, A Series of Sketches* (New York, 1853); Calhoun, J. C.: *Works* (Charleston, 1851, New York, 1853-5); Cooper, Thos.: *Consolidation: An Account of Parties in the United States, from the Convention of 1787 to the Present Period* (published anonymously, Columbia, 1824), and *Lectures on the Elements of Political Economy* (Columbia, 1826); DeBow, J. D. B.: *The Industrial Resources, etc., of the Southern and Western States* (New Orleans, 1853-4); Dunning, W. A.: *American Political Philosophy* (in the *Yale Reveiw*, August, 1895); Elliott, E. N.: *Cotton Is King and Pro-Slavery Arguments Comprising the Writings of Hammond, Harper, Christy, Stringfellow, Hodge, Bledsoe, and Cartwright on This Important Subject* (Augusta, 1860); Fitzhugh, Geo.: *Cannibals All, or Slaves Without Masters* (Richmond, 1857), and *Sociology for the South, or The Failure of Free Society* (Richmond, 1854); Fletcher, John: *Studies on Slavery in Easy Lessons* (Natchez, 1852); Goodloe, D. R.: *Inquiry into the Causes which have Retarded the Accumulation of Wealth and Increase of Population in the Southern States* (Washington, 1846). (This essay is said by S. B. Weeks to have been written in 1841; it was published first in the *New York American*, 1844, and in several places thereafter); Gregg, Wm.: *Essays on Domestic Industry, or an Inquiry into the Expediency of Establishing Cotton Manufactures in South Carolina* (Charleston, 1845); Harper, Robert Goodloe: *Select Works* (Baltimore, 1814); [Harrison, Jesse Burton]: *Review of the Slave Question, Extracted from the American Quarterly Review, December,* 1832, *Showing That Slavery is a Hindrance to Prosperity*, by a Virginian (Richmond, 1833); Helper, H. R.: *The Impending Crisis of the South: How to*

Meet It (New York, 1857), and *Nojoque, A Question for a Continent* (New York, 1867); Houston, D. F · *A Critical Study of Nullification in South Carolina* (New York, 1896); Hughes, Henry *State Liberties: The Right to African Contract Labor* (Port Gibson, Miss , 1858); Hundley, D. R : *Social Relations in Our Southern States* (New York, 1860), Ingle, Edward, *Southern Sidelights* (New York, 1896); Merriam, C E.· *The Political Theory of Calhoun* (in the *American Journal of Sociology*, VII., 577–594); Nott, Josiah, C.· *Two Lectures on the Natural History of the Caucasian and Negro Races* (Mobile, 1844); Phillips, U. B . *The Slave Labor Problem in the Charleston District* (in the *Political Science Quarterly*, XXII , 416–439); *The Pro-Slavery Argument, as maintained by the Most Distinguished Writers of the Southern States, Containing the Several Essays on the Subject, of Chancellor Harper, Governor Hammond, Dr. Simms and Professor Dew* (Charleston, 1852); Ruffin, Edmund. *An Address on the Opposite Results of Exhausting and Fertilizing Systems of Agriculture* (Charleston, 1853), *Calcareous Manures* (2d ed., 1835) and *Report of the Commencement and Progress of the Agricultural Survey of South Carolina for 1843* (Columbia, 1843); Sawyer, Geo. S.: *Southern Institutes* (Philadelphia, 1858); Seabrook, Whitemarsh B.: *A Memoir on the Origin, Cultivation and Uses of Cotton* (Charleston, 1844), Simms, W. G *Southward Ho! A Spell of Sunshine* (New York, 1854); Taylor, John, of Caroline: *Arator, Being a Series of Agricultural Essays, Practical and Political*, by a citizen of Virginia (anonymously published) (Georgetown, D. C., 1813), *Construction Construed* (1822), *Inquiry Into the Principles and Policy of the Government of the United States* (Fredericksburg, 1814), *New Views of the Constitution* (1823) and *Tyranny Unmasked* (Washington, 1822); Trescott, W. H . *The Position and Course of the South* (Charleston, 1850); Tucker, George *Essays on Various Subjects of Taste, Morals and National Policy*, by a citizen of Virginia (published anonymously) (Georgetown, D. C , 1822), and *The Theory of Money and Banks Investigated* (Boston, 1839); Tucker, St. George. *Dissertation on Slavery, With a Proposal for Its Gradual Abolition in Virginia* (Philadelphia, 1796, reprinted New York, 1861); Weeks, Stephen B *Anti-Slavery Sentiment in the South* (in the *Southern History Association Publications*, II , 87–130); Weston, George M.: *The Progress of Slavery in the United States* (Washington, 1857).

ULRICH B. PHILLIPS,
Professor of History, Tulane University.

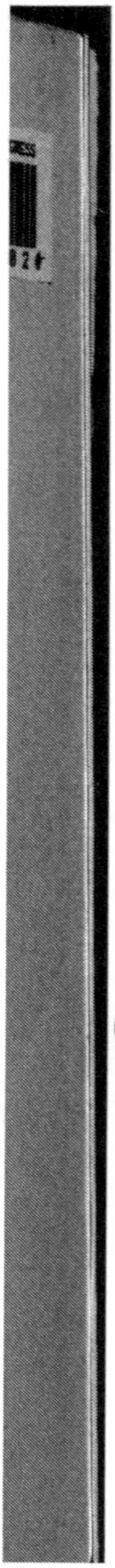

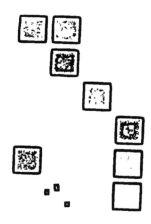

Lightning Source UK Ltd.
Milton Keynes UK
UKHW021126270120
357678UK00009B/2459